SELLING STONE COUNTERTOPS

A Sales Guide for
Countertop Fabricators

Thomas Robinson

Selling Stone Countertops

"Nothing happens until somebody sells something."
Arthur H. (Red) Motley
1930

Copyright © 2012 Thomas Robinson

All rights reserved. No part of this book may be reproduced or transmitted by any means electronic or mechanical, including photocopying, recording, retrieval system without written permission from the author and the publisher (except brief quotations in reviews).

Thomas Robinson

Selling Stone Countertops

To the Board of Directors

and Other Volunteers of the

Stone Fabricators Alliance

"The Stone Fabricator's Alliance is an organization comprised of fabrication and restoration professionals from around the world. Its objective is to provide the resources necessary to enable members to prosper by improving their quality of fabrication and restoration methods and practices. It does this by sharing information, skills and techniques – all for the good of the hardworking professionals that make up this industry."

Thomas Robinson

CONTENTS

Sales is Like a Beer Wagon 10

Introduction to First Edition 15

Create Your Own Process 18

Clean Up Your Production 19

Unique Selling Proposition (USP) for Stone...22

Identify (Profile) Your Target Customer 25

Prospecting: Six Ways To Get More Prospects....................................27

Building Rapport..30

Determine the Decision Maker 31

Determine Needs 32

Qualify the Customer 35

Determine Budget 36

Selling Features and Benefits 38

The Presentation 40

Overcoming Objections...41

Overcoming the Price Objection: Is It the Real Issue? 43

Ask for the Order...46

Quoting Price on the Phone 48

Follow Up and Ask for Referrals 50

Things You Need To Know About Your Customer 52

Things You Need To Know About Your Market...................................54

Things You Need to Know About Salespeople 55

The Hardest Thing in Sales 56

Four Positive Outcomes of a Sales Call 58

Working Home Shows and Trade Shows: Part 1 60

Working Home Shows and Trade Shows: Part 2 62

I Hear You 64

Keep the Prospect Engaged 66

The Pitch 68

Be a Consultant 70

Finding Out What Makes People Buy 72

Why Do Your Customers Buy From You? 74

Who Owns the Customer: Part 1 76

Who Owns the Customer: Part 2 78

Conclusion 80

APPENDICES 81

How to Buy the Cheapest Granite Countertop 81

The Scandal of the Free Sink 83

How to Maintain Your Stone Countertop 85

Granite, Marble and Other Stones 86

The Marble Institute 89

Ten Questions to Ask Your Customers 90

Ten responses to "What's Your Square-Foot Price?" 92

Thomas Robinson

The ideas in this booklet are not original.

Much of the techniques and strategies I use in my career came from the sales giants who have shared their experiences in books and tapes on sales – some of which are listed at the back of this booklet. I also drew from my own experiences as a business owner and salesperson.

Much of the information on the stone countertop industry has come from my customers who have permitted me to share their experience and knowledge. To those customers, I am grateful. This particularly applies to the section on prospecting.

There are, of course, other sales methods and techniques that I have not shared because I did not get permission.

I am always looking for new sales techniques and look forward to hearing from you.

Tom Robinson
trobinson725@gmail.com

Thomas Robinson

Sales is Like a Beer Wagon

Sales is like the beer wagons we see in the commercials during the last football game of the year. You need four big strong Clydesdales to pull your beer wagon. Three horses or even three horses and a pony will not successfully pull your wagon. Like the beer wagon, your sales program has four components that work as a team and are co-dependent and interrelated.

The first component is a **quality product**. Quality is defined as a product that meets the needs and expectations of the consumer. If you are selling a car to a college student whose primary concern is that he does not need to put too much of his beer money in the gas tank and it will get him home once a month to see his girlfriend, then a 3-year-old economy car is a quality product. But if you are selling a car to a wealthy doctor who wants to impress his friends, neighbors, colleagues and even himself, then you likely need to offer an imported luxury car.

Obviously, the "quality" level is different in a 3-year-old economy car and a new imported luxury car but each is quality to the consumer. Not only do you need to offer the right level of quality to the right customer but to maintain your sales program long term, you need to be honest with your customer and yourself about what you are selling. You cannot offer an economy car and sell it as a luxury car. It might work once but not in the long term. When I was selling homes, we had a saying: "Sell the sizzle not the steak." However, if you sell the sizzle you still have to make sure you have a steak. Selling the sizzle without a steak to back it up is fraud.

The second component of your sales program is a **good sales attitude and company culture**. Sales is a necessary process. Without sales, there will be no product to make, no books to keep and no products to purchase. The company will fail and all production staff, bookkeeper, purchasing agent and all the rest of employees will lose their jobs.

Not only do the salespeople have to have a good attitude, but everyone who works for the company must understand that they are part of the sales process and need to work together on sales. If the salespeople come back to production with a quality or fashion issue, the production staff must be open to making changes or adjustments. If they take the attitude that they have made widgets the same way for 10 years without making improvements along the way, then it will impact quality and sales.

What can you do about improving your sales attitude and company culture?

- Keep the customer's interest your highest priority. If your product is not the right product for the customer or you cannot meet their needs, do not proceed. If you keep the customer's interest first, two magical things happen;
    - First, you feel better about the process and your position as a salesperson.
    - And second, you will generate more sales.
- Understand that sales is a honorable profession. Nearly every book, CD or seminar on sales includes a chapter dedicated to convincing the reader, listener or attendee that sales is an honorable profession. No other group of employees, bookkeepers, purchasing agents or production staff needs to be convinced their job is honorable. Sales is not an option and if done right, it is both honorable and rewarding. Without sales, the

bookkeeper, the purchasing agent and production staff will all lose their jobs and the company will fail.
- Realize that if you have a quality product that meets your customers' needs, it is your duty to get it into the hands of the people it will most likely benefit. Of course, you first need to make sure you have a quality product. There is no way to feel good about selling a product your customer does not need or want.
- Make sales a full-time activity. You do not ask your production staff to do the bookkeeping or answer the phones. Why would you ask the bookkeeper or receptionist to do sales? If your bookkeeper is doing sales, then sales is an interruption from the activities that the bookkeeper uses to define himself or herself. If an employee has the choice between routine easy tasks such as entering invoices into a computer and hard necessary tasks such as cold calling and follow-up calls, the employee will always do the routine easy tasks that he/she defines as part of their job. If they start entering a stack of bills into a computer, by the end of the day they will have accomplished something. If they make the cold calls or follow up calls, he/she might be rejected, told no or otherwise reach unsuccessful results. This bookkeeper or other employee will likely have a poor attitude toward sales.
- And finally, you need to identify the weak parts of your sales process so you can work to improve them. If you shore up the weak parts, all employees involved in the process will feel more comfortable and perform better. Success will then, in turn, improve attitude.

The third component of your sales program is **sales skills**. You need to know how to prospect, build rapport, determine needs, make sales presentations, close the sale and more. From the most basic to the subtle the skills are available if you are willing to go out and find them. It takes work *not* because they are hard to find, but because there is so much information available that you need to find the skills that are right for your industry and your personality.

There are books, CDs, seminars and videos by some giants in the sales training field such as Zig Ziglar, Tom Hopkins, Brian Tracy and many others. Find the method of delivery that is most effective for you.

You do not need to spend a fortune. I started with a local library. For me, the best way to pass the many hours I spend staring at my windshield is listening to recordings of books and seminars. You can find many of these available on YouTube for free. I download them, convert to audio and listen as I travel.

You need to listen over and over because each time you will hear something you missed before or understand something you heard in a new way. The third or fourth time, you may understand something and how it applies to you, your customers or your industry that you missed before.

Motivational recordings are also important to salespeople. It is hard to stay motivated. Listening to a motivational recording each morning can help you be where you need to be. Even listening to upbeat music on the way to a difficult sales call can be very helpful to get you in a mood for success.

The final component of a great sales program is a **sales process**. When you produce your product or service, it is likely you have a process that you follow. Even if it is not written down, you can likely describe what it takes to make your product. If you are building a house, you have a construction schedule to follow. If you are repairing cars, you have a process for diagnosing each problem, ordering the parts, making the repair and double checking to make sure the repair was done correctly and solved the problem.

Sales is just like that. You need to have a process to follow. If you have a process, you know what to do next and you can identify what is working, continue to use the technique. You will also be able to identify where your procedure is weak or nonexistent and you can create what you are missing or work on what is weak. A process will also help keep you on track and ensure you are not skipping the parts with which you are uncomfortable.

Thomas Robinson

Introduction to First Edition

Sales, more than anything else, is about attitude.

ANO, Inc. had a salesman a few years ago. One of his duties was to make cold calls on countertop fabricators to find prospects for our sinks and faucets. No salesperson likes to make cold calls and most make up justification to delay or avoid the process. This salesperson told me he did not need to make sales calls on many fabricators because he could tell they would not buy just by driving by their shop. It seems he got so good at knowing who would not buy he could do it from the golf course because that is where he spent many of the hours he was suppose to be prospecting. He was absolutely correct. Every prospect he did not visit did not buy.

**The Number One Rule in Small Business Sales is:
You do not need to like it but you do need to do it!**

Sales is about determining what customers need and want, **then** fitting your product into their needs and wants. Find out what the customer wants and give it to them. Make them want it <u>before</u> you talk price and you will close more sales.

Why do most business owners hate sales?

1. Salespeople in general have a very poor reputation, much of it earned. It is easy to dislike many salespeople. The problem is that too many sales practitioners are not professionals but merely long-time amateurs who occasionally stumble on a sale. A true salesperson does <u>not</u> have slicked back hair, wears shiny suits, or sports lots of "bling." A true salesperson does not lie, push or

misrepresent. A true salesperson dresses like their customer, is polite and helpful and always places the **customer's interest** *first*.
2. Many business owners started on the production side of the business. They started the business because they could make stuff better – not because they could sell stuff better. More often than not, they fought with the sales people as the production concerns conflicted with the desires of the sales department.
3. **If a business owner hates sales,** it is unlikely they dislike *everything* about sales. It is more likely they hate the preconceived image they have about salespeople or they hate some part of the process. Maybe they like talking to the customers but they hate overcoming objections. When I owned my home building business, I was able to close eight out of 10 prospects with whom I talked. The problem was I did not have enough prospects because I was not comfortable prospecting. I worked on every part of my sales process except the part I really needed to work on.

Here are six truths about small business sales every small business owner must understand.
1. Sales is an honorable profession. I am a student of the sales process. I have over 100 CDs on sales I listen to as I travel around the Midwest. All of these programs and nearly every book I have read on the subject begins with a section dedicated to convincing the listener or reader that sales is a honorable profession. I wonder if the practitioners of any other profession have to be convinced that they are involved in an honorable profession? Do you suppose that seminars for brain surgeons, rocket scientists or bus drivers start with a few paragraphs on how honorable their profession is? Why do you suppose some salespeople hide behind titles like

2. "designer," "associate," "consultant," or "business development professional?"
3. Sales is *not* an option. If you are in business, you are in sales. Without sales, the best stone countertop on the planet will never get sold. All the company employees from receptionist, accountant, fabricator and installer will be out of work and the company will fail. Not because of production, purchasing, bookkeeping or any other department, but because there are no countertops to produce, products to purchase or accounts to balance. You do not need to like sales, but you need to do it.
4. If you make a good product, it is your duty to get it into the hands of consumers who would benefit from such a countertop.
5. You need to work on the parts of your sales process that are hard for you as well as the parts that are easy.
6. Sales in not a part-time activity. You do not ask your lead fabricator to answer the phone, greet people who come into your office or do bookkeeping. Why would you ask your salesperson to do these activities or worse, why would you have your receptionist or bookkeeper do sales? It is easier to do the routine things rather than the hard things such as cold calling and follow up. Given the choice, an employee will do easy routine tasks instead of hard important ones. They will look busy instead of doing things that lead to a sale.
7. Nothing happens until somebody sells something.

Create Your Own Process

Why do we need a process?

Success in sales can happen by mistake. You can do everything wrong and you still make a sale. BUT – it is better if you do the *right* things at the *right* time. Having an established process helps keep you on track and it helps you improve what works and dump what does not.

1. Clean up your process so you can deliver the customer a positive experience from the first time they contact you until the top is in their home and they forget it was not always there.
2. Develop a Unique Selling Proposition (USP).
3. Identify the customers who are most profitable for your company.
4. Prospect for customers who fit the profile you create.
5. Build rapport with the prospect.
6. Determine the decision maker.
7. Determine the needs and wants of the customer by questioning them about what they want and need.
8. Qualify the customer.
9. Determine the customer's budget.
10. Make a custom presentation that addresses the prospect's wants and needs.
11. Ask for the business.
12. Deliver the product memorably so the customer will want to buy, buy again and give you referrals.
13. Follow up to make sure that the product is what you promised and get referrals.

Clean Up Your Production

At Disney World there is a sign just outside the locker room where all the employees, or "cast members," dress.

The sign says, "Take Pride in the Product."

They understand that even if the cast member is having a bad day or does not feel like putting on the best show, that their customer is here on vacation. It might be a once-in-a-lifetime experience for the guest and it is imperative that the show be fresh and exciting every time so the guest goes home and tells all their friends about their experience.

What is your product? Wrong. Your product is not just a stone countertop. It is a better brighter kitchen or a kitchen better than the Jones', or a fulfillment of a dream. It is the CUSTOMER'S entire experience from the day someone from your company first speaks with them up to the day when the customer is using the countertop and forgets that it was not always there.

Your job is to make that experience superior and to make the customer happy they chose your company, used the countertop then forgot about you ... until someone asks them who did the work.

If you produce an excellent or even a superior countertop but were three weeks late, did not communicate with your customer, and left a mess, then you will not get repeat business or referrals. You may never hear a complaint from the customer but the customer's friends and relatives – *your prospects* – certainly will.

The countertop you produce will be in the customer's home for a very long time. It will represent you, so it needs to be superior even if you or your employees were having a bad day when they were making the top. And as long as your customer is in the home, they will remember the experience as well, particularly if it was bad and pass it on.

You need to clean up your production process first. Some things you need to consider as you clean up your process.

1. Do you make the best countertop that you can produce? Do you use the best materials or just good enough materials? Are you proud of the product?
2. How is your phone answered and how it is answered when no one is there?
3. How does the showroom look? Is it neat and clean? I regularly see dusty and dirty showrooms because there is a door to the shop right in the showroom.
4. Are your salespeople on time for appointments, available when the customer needs them and professional in appearance and actions?
5. Is your slab selection process customer friendly? If you are sending your prospects to a wholesale stone supplier unsupervised, some of them will be stolen.
6. Are your edge and accessory samples clean, helpful and do they accurately represent the work you do?
7. How is your scheduling system? Is it accurate or are you often calling customers to reschedule? Communicate your schedule to the customer and most important – delays and reasons for delay.
8. Define quality for your work and live up to those standards.
9. Respect the customer's home. Make sure your tradesmen do not damage the home bringing in the countertop. Make sure they are dressed appropriately and clean. Make sure they do not smoke, use colorful language or do anything in the home they would not do if they were a guest in the house. Leave the home cleaner than when your workmen arrive. Make sure they have proper

cleaning equipment: broom, rags, cleaning solutions and shop vacuum.
10. Follow up to make sure the customer received everything they were promised and ask for referrals. My wife and I recently had to have several trees removed after a storm. The tree service did a fine job except they never finished removing the debris as they promised. We left a message at the office but did not hear back from them. Several neighbors who saw the truck working in our yard called and asked for a reference. We told them they did good work but never finished as promised. None of them hired the tree service. The tree service never heard the complaint but lost several jobs because they did not finish and make the experience superior.
11. You need to make sure that you are able to deliver a superior product <u>and</u> experience or your competition will.
12. Do not assume that because you are not getting complaints that you are not losing business.

Unique Selling Proposition (USP) for Stone

I know of three stone fabricators that have all done business for years on the same block in a midsize town in Wisconsin. After years of a peaceful co-existence, the market got tough and one of the shops decided to put a sign in the window that read: "We make the best stone countertop is **town**."

Not to be outdone, the second shop soon put a sign in its window proclaiming: "We make the best stone countertops in **Wisconsin**."

Finally, the third shop put a sign in its window that read: "We make the best stone countertops on the **block**."

Entrepreneur magazine defines Unique Selling Proposition as: "The factor or consideration presented by a seller as the reason that one product or service is different from and better than that of the competition. Your USP is the reason your customer buys from you and not your competition."

- You need to find a unique selling proposition that gives your prospects a reason to buy from you. It is best if your competition cannot easily or quickly duplicate your USP.
- Without a USP, the prospect can only make their decision based on price.
- To develop your USP you need to understand what you do that is different than your competition.
- If you have a number of different kinds of competition you may need to develop several different USPs to deal with each of the different types.

Selling Stone Countertops

Possible USPs:

- Do you have a unique way of making tops that your competition cannot duplicate? A CNC machine when no one else in your market has one can be your USP. But hand craftsmanship in a market where everything is done by computer can also be used as a USP. You just have to develop the strategy.
- Do you have unique polishing processes?
- Do you the largest or most unique selection of slabs in your market?
- Is your process of helping the consumer design their kitchen or select their slabs such as having a designer accompany the consumer to the slab wholesaler different or unique?
- Have you won awards? Awards are great because they take some of the risk of the purchase out of the process.
- Does your company or staff have more experience than the competition? For example: "Our staff has an average of 20 years experience."
- Do you or your staff have unique certification or training by manufacturers?
- Do you have fast turnaround or boast, "We take longer because we have so many satisfied customers and we take the time to do it right?"
- Develop a checklist that consumers should look for from a countertop fabricator so they can distinguish you from the garage fabricators. Even if you do not get the job, it will make the cheap guys' job harder. If you do not have one, send me an email and I will send you a copy of our blog post, "How to Buy the Cheapest Granite Countertop."
- Some other USPs might be *unique* accessories, *special* accessories, *special* sealers, etc.

If you use any variation of quality such as *best stone countertop in town*, you better be ready to define quality and make sure you meet your own standards. Better quality is not a USP unless you can define it and prove it.

Avoid price! You cannot afford to be the cheapest in town and if you advertise price, you will attract the wrong kind of buyer.

Identify (Profile) Your Target Customer

Make a list of your best customers. What made them good customers? Where do they live? What age group are they in? Where do they hang out?

If you can identify your best customers and create a profile, then you can go out and look for customers just like them.

If you have several great customers from a particular area, a particular size home, or a particular age home, then you may be able to look in those same areas for new great customers.

For example, if there is a nearby town that has homes that are 20-30 years old and are due for remodeling and upgrades, it is a better place to look than a 1-year-old subdivision where everything is new.

The reverse is also true. You do not need to redline, which means refuse to work in certain areas but if there is a town where unemployment is very high and property values are falling, it might not be the place to prospect. If you do get a prospect, make sure they can afford to pay you.

Some things to look for:
- Age group.
- Income range.
- Age of home.
- Value of home.
- How long the prospect has owned the home.
- Rising or sinking home values in area.
- Retired.

- Marital status.
- Type of employment.
- Club membership.
- Age of children/grade in school.

Once you understand what kind of customer is best for you, look for that customer and tailor your product to serve that profile.

You can also develop profiles for customers that are a problem for you. When we were building homes, we used to hate lawyers because it took longer to do the contract than build the home.

Prospecting: Six Ways To Get More Prospects

Every business needs a source of new customers. Advertising, home shows, word of mouth. By the way, referrals are word-of-mouth on steroids.

Here are six methods my customers tell me they use to find more prospects.

They are not easy. They take work. But they will get you new customers.

1. Advertise the lowest price in town. This has two advantages. This is the easiest and you will not need many customers because you will not be in business long. Ignore this idea.
2. Make sure that your end product and all phases of your process make the customer's buying experience superior so the customer will want more and will want to recommend you to others. Make sure your entire staff understands that they are in sales and their most important job is to give the customer an exceptional experience and product.
3. Create a maintenance instruction sheet for your product. Do not leave it with the countertop but mail it. *Even better*: deliver it to the customer about three weeks after the installation. If you leave it with the customer when you install the top it will likely get thrown out when the work area is cleaned. Make the instructions valuable and the card attractive enough that the customer wants to keep it. Having it laminated gives it importance and your customer is more likely to keep it. Attach several of your cards to the instructions with two-sided tape. When your customer's friends and neighbors come to visit and

admire the new kitchen, they can pull out the instruction sheets and give them your card. If you do not have maintenance instructions of your own there is one in the Appendix.
4. When you visit to drop off the maintenance instructions, ask for referrals. Ask if the customer will call likely prospects for you and recommend you or at least give you a written referral. Getting them to recommend you on Angie's list can be particularly productive. Email them pictures of their kitchen and ask them to post it on their Facebook page or other social media sites.
5. Take pictures of each project. Send out a postcard to "neighbors" that reads, "One of your neighbors just updated their home with a new stone top from XYZ Granite. Would you like to see pictures?" The postcard should have a professional picture of one of your best projects. There is no size definition for neighborhood so send it to as large an area as you think you can handle at one time. This is particularly effective if you have a subdivision of similar homes. You can add wording such as "We just completed a new kitchen in a Hampton Model." Prospects will want to know what their home could look like. Mailings have a very low percentage of return but adding the neighborhood factor and pictures will add an "affinity" hook that will increase return. You can also go door-to-door with your pictures. There are no "no knock" laws.
6. Send a postcard to past customers reminding them you are still serving their area and ask for repeat business (suggest a bathroom if you did the kitchen, for example) or referrals.
7. When you send out a crew to measure a kitchen top, have them measure all the bathrooms, bars, etc, even if these items are not part of this project. You now have the information to quote these items either with the current

order or as a follow up. If the customer seems reluctant, simply inform them that this way the information will be on file if they decide to change these other tops in the future.

I sent this list to a customer of mine who complained he was not busy. By return email he sent me the message, "Nothing new here." So I called him and said, "The ideas are not new but are you doing them?" He said, "Well, no." I then told him even old ideas will not work if you do not use them.

These are not the only ways to prospect for customers. Be careful with advertising, though. Even if you do not mention price, it is perceived to be price-based by the consumer.

Home shows, if you work them, can be valuable because they attract prospects looking to buy. But you need to have a strategy and work the show – not just sit and hope prospects come to you. And you need to follow up on the leads you do receive. Word of mouth is OK, but remember – referrals are word-of-mouth on steroids.

Building Rapport

Rapport is a connection or a sympathetic relation. Building rapport is a critical part of the sales process. Salespeople sometimes refer to the process as "selling yourself first."

People buy from people, so it is important to make a connection to the prospect. If you have a showroom and a new prospect comes in, the worst thing you can say is "Can I help you?" Consumers are programmed to say "no" when asked this question upon entering a retail store. Don't believe it? See what happens next time you go into a retail store and someone asks that question.

Instead, find a way to engage the prospect such as, "Hi, I'm Sally Sales Lady. Welcome to our design center where we specialize in updating and upgrading kitchens to add value to our customer's home. Do you live in the area?"

This gets them engaged and talking instead of shutting down. Develop follow up questions that get them talking, such as "How did you hear about us?"

If you are making a sales call to a home, make a sincere comment on something you like in their house.

Take a few minutes to bond but do it sincerely and do not overdo it. If you fake it, the customer will know. If you do too much, then the customer will feel you are either wasting their time or you are not confident in your presentation.

Once you establish rapport, make sure you keep a record of what you learned and said. Covering the same ground again in the future might undo what rapport you built.

Determine the Decision Maker

It does no good to sell to someone who cannot say "yes." Early in your process, you must determine who and how the prospect will make a decision. If you are talking to only the wife or husband or only half of any relationship, you need find out how the decision will be made.

A great way to ask is, "Who beside yourself will be involved in this decision?" or "How does your family make these kinds of purchases?"

If only one party says "I make all the decisions," it might be wise to ask later in the conversation, "Who will be helping you with this decision?" You might get the same reply or you might get, "My wife/mother/sister/son/friend/decorator usually helps me make decisions like this."

Whoever is involved in the decision, it's best to get them all involved when you present the solution. If decision makers or major influencers are not engaged in the presentation, you will not have an opportunity to overcome objections.

Suggest you schedule an appointment when all the decision makers and influencers can be present. That does not mean you need to rent out an auditorium to give the presentation. One or two advisors are plenty.

Along the same lines, make sure you have the decision maker's attention when presenting your solution. If they bring all 10 kids to the meeting, politely suggest you reschedule when they can arrange for someone to watch the kids.

Determine Needs

Excessive soap-boxing can kill rapport. Once you establish rapport, you can spill your guts and vomit everything you know about your product. In case the language is not colorful enough and you do not get it, talking is the worst thing you can do. What you need to do is ask questions to determine what they want or help them discover what they want. **Selling is about asking – not telling.** By letting prospects talk, you earn their trust and the right to present your solution.

Use your experience to create questions that can lead to what the customer wants and needs. It is critical to listen to the answers. Make notes. It will make the prospect feel important and impress them that you are listening.

Sample questions might be:

1. What do you hope to accomplish with this project? Brighter? More durable? Easier to clean? Updated kitchen? Change in layout? Add something such as breakfast bar?
2. How long do you intend to be in your home? Is this a long-term investment or are you just installing a new top to sell the home?
3. What kind of countertop do you have now and what do you like about it?
4. Why do you think you want a stone top?
5. What do you know about stone tops and what are your expectations? What have you heard from family or friends about their stone tops? What do they say they would do if they did it again? What would they not do? What did they tell you about the remodeling experience?

Selling Stone Countertops

6. Do you like unique things? Would you like a countertop that is different from everyone else's or would you prefer it look just like the sample?
7. How do you use the countertop?
8. What do you dislike about your current top?
9. Are there things in your home that might impact the countertop selection? If you have very hard water with a lot of minerals, for example, a black granite top might be hard to keep clean.

Ask questions that help you discover which of your products will best fit the prospects' needs.

After you ask the appropriate questions, make sure you SHUT UP and listen.

Resist the temptation to start selling before you complete the process. Ask and shut up. It is the hardest thing to do in sales. Answer questions with questions. If the prospect asks "Will it be ready by Christmas?" before you jump in with how you can get it to them by Christmas, make sure you ask questions to develop the reason behind the remark. "Do you want it by Christmas?"

They may say "Yes, we are having a big party." Or they may say "No, we do not get our bonus until January and we want to wait until then." If you jump in before you develop what they need, you could be selling to the wrong desire.

In the early '90s, we were building townhome-style duplexes in Hoffman Estates, Illinois. We were just a few miles from Sears' new, huge headquarters. We were trying very hard to target some of the employees moving to the new facility, hoping they would spread the word about their new home.

Our salesperson, Betty, was a seasoned new home sales rep and real estate agent. She was very excited when a women being transferred into the new Sears facility visited our project several times. This buyer was considering our project and another in a neighboring town. Our homes were larger and closer to her job. She said she liked our layout better. The only issue: All our units had basements and she did not want a basement.

Betty used her experience to translate that to mean she could not afford or at least did not want to pay for a basement she would not use. Betty reported this to the owners of the project, who worked with Betty to put together a package of discounts, credits and special financing that eliminated the premium for the basement.

After several weeks of working with the buyer, Betty received the call she never expected. Her customer had purchased the other home. Betty was so disturbed by the lost sale she went to see the unit that the woman had purchased. It was smaller, it backed up to an arterial road and Betty was certain our layout and standard features were better. Worst of all, the unit was more expensive even without the discount package for the basement.

Betty was so confused by the customer's choice she was sure she understood, she called the customer to congratulate her on her new purchase and ask her the rationale behind her decision. In response, the lost customer replied, "I told you I didn't want a basement."

Betty then asked the question that never occurred to her before, "Why don't you want a basement?" The woman then explained that Sears has a very good warranty program on their sump pumps. She worked in the warranty department and any time there was a sump pump failure, she got the call. She had heard so many horror stories about sump pumps, she decided she would never buy a home with a basement.

Do no rush this step! Make sure you not only find out that they do not want a basement, but also *why* they do not want a basement.

Qualify the Customer

Another important thing to remember during the entire process but particularly in the determining needs and wants stage is this: you need to be qualifying the prospect. Are your countertops a good fit for this customer and is this customer going to be a profitable for your company?

Are the husband and wife fighting during the entire process? If so, it is unlikely you can make them happy. An unhappy customer is usually unprofitable and will cost you more in reputation than you can profit on the project.

Listen for problem indicators. I had a prospect looking to buy a home from me. The husband indicated that he wanted to have a completion penalty clause in his contract because he had problems with a previous builder.

He would not tell me who the builder was but from his address I figured it out. I knew the builder from the home builders association and he had an excellent reputation. I called up the builder and asked what he remembered about this prospect. He said "Do not walk away... RUN. The prospect never made his product selections on time and delayed the project. He then wanted a penalty when the home was not finished on time." He also said the couple was very difficult, demanding and unprofitable.

You get 80% of your problems from 20% of your customers. If you can eliminate problems early, you will have more time for profitable customers. The 80/20 rule is not just an old wives' tale. It even has a name. It is called the Pareto principle. It is also known as the 80-20 rule, the law of the vital few, and the principle of factor sparsity.

Determine Budget

Before you can create a presentation and proposal for the prospect, it is critical you determine and understand the prospect's budget and expectations. What can they spend and what <u>will</u> they spend. It may be two different things.

With all the low stone countertop prices being advertised, your prospect may come into the conversation with unrealistic expectations. The sooner you figure out that they are expecting to do their marble kitchen based on the price they saw on a lawn sign, the better off you are.

Nothing is worse than getting to the end of a great presentation to find out the prospect cannot or will not pay for your product.

What is their budget? You have to ask!

"Do you have a budget for this project?" Or, "What were you hoping to spend on this remodel?"

No one wants to overspend but if you cannot do what they want for the budget they have, it is better to stop now and not waste both your time and the prospect's time.

Sometimes they will not want to tell you a budget so you need to help them. "Were you expecting to be in the $3,000 to $6,000 range or $6,000 to $12,000 range?" Scale the ranges to the project but do not under-price. If they say "No, we want to spend less than that," then test the statement with, "If we came up with the perfect kitchen for you could you go as high as $xxx? Or say simply and firmly, "That will be a problem." And wait until they reply.

<u>Do not continue</u> until both you and the prospect understand the scope of the project and the budget with which you are working.

If they tell you that they saw a sign for $24 a square foot and they measured and they know they have 25 square feet, you can begin to sell against the unrealistic price. At least warn them about what they might get for that price.

The second part of the budget step is determining how they intend to pay for the project. If the prospect has the cash, they are unlikely to be offended by the question. If they do not have a plan, now is the time to discover it. "We require a 50% deposit with all orders. Is that a problem?"

Do not waste your time chasing an unrealistic budget or a customer who cannot pay.

Selling Features and Benefits

Traditional selling systems are based on selling features and benefits. There is an excellent reason so many systems are based on features and benefits and that is because it works ... to a point.

A feature is a characteristic of the product. For example, the house has a premium upgraded roof. The benefits might be articulated like, "The shingles are sculptured to look like natural wood shingles and they have a 40-year warranty that will outlast your mortgage." Both are benefits using the traditional selling methods.

Salespeople are taught to present features and benefits to prospects with linking phrases such as *which means* or *the benefits are*. "The house has a premium roof, *which means* the shingles are sculpted to provide the rich look of natural wood shingles and the roof has a 40-year warranty." The *benefit is* "The warranty will last longer than your mortgage."

Make a list of the features of your product. Make sure you include all of them in your presentation. It is easy to miss features that you know about because they are so common, assuming the customer must already know. If you are selling granite countertops, a feature might be "Granite is the hardest material in nature." You might have been working with the product so long that the fact that granite is hard may seem like common knowledge to you but it might not be to your customer. The feature and benefit might become, "Our countertops are made from granite, the hardest material in nature, which means it will last a lifetime in your kitchen."

The problem with features and benefits selling is that it can be incorrectly used. If you are selling a product with a 40-

year warranty and the customer intends to only keep the house for five years, the 40-year warranty seems like a waste of money. If you emphasize that countertops are made of long-lasting hard granite, that consumer may worry they will break their plates on it.

Your product has features and advantages. Advantages are what traditional selling systems call benefits. However, an advantage is not a benefit unless it is a benefit to this particular prospect. In the needs determination process, you should discover which of the advantages are *benefits* to your prospect. By presenting only the advantages that are benefits to your particular prospect, your prospect will feel like your product, no matter how standard, is custom designed for them. It also reduces the possibility of presenting what you believe is a benefit but actually a negative to the customer.

The key to this process, like so much of your sales processes, is to spend enough quality time discovering true needs to present the right benefits.

The Presentation

If you have done the process right up to this point, the presentation of the solution should be the easiest part. As the saying goes, "Find out what the customer wants and give it to them."

You should now know what they want, what problems they have had in the past, which of your products most closely solves the problem they have had and what they are willing and able to spend on the project. You know what they want. Give it to them... *if you can*. If you can't, it is time to back out.

Before you make your presentation, list the needs and wants they told you.

For example: "You said your kitchen is too dark, you need a breakfast area that your kids can use to do homework ..." then continue to list all the things that the customer wants and finish by saying, "and your budget is approximately $xxx, is that right?" If you get an agreement at this point and you can meet all the wants within the budget, you will have a very good chance of getting the order.

DO NOT GIVE A PRICE until you have gotten an agreement that your solution meets their wants and needs. You need to have the prospect *want* the solution before you give a final price. If you get ahead of yourself and give a price before you have an agreement, you lose and will likely lose the order. If you have options, then price them separately but do not give out a price until *after* you have gotten them on board.

Overcoming Objections

You likely already know what objections your prospects have to your product. Make a list of those common objections. Usually there are about 10. Prepare a script for all common objections so you are prepared and can sound professional and knowledgeable. By knowing the script, you will be able to concentrate on the prospect's reactions as you present the script and know how to react. Practice the script until it becomes second nature.

You can often overcome objections by dealing with them in your presentation. If your product has a weakness that you often hear, try and include overcoming this objection in your presentation.

I had a customer who had a long lead time to make and deliver countertops because he was so busy. Another countertop fabricator began advertising "Installation within a week." My customer in his presentation would talk about the many steps they took in preparing and fabricating the countertop. He also pointed out in the presentation that because he took such good care of his customers, they often referred their friends and neighbors. These referrals were causing their lead time to be as long as six weeks. They also told their prospects that no matter how busy they were, they never rushed the process. They wanted to make sure all their customers were satisfied enough to willingly give referrals. Not only did this overcome the objections before it was voiced, but it reinforced their efforts to produce high quality countertops.

If a prospect *does* bring up an objection, do not take it personally. Make sure you listen and understand the objection completely. Ask follow-up questions like, "What do you mean by that?" or "Can you tell me more about that?"

It will be very tempting to launch into your prepared script and overcome the objection as soon as you THINK you understand the objection. Note the objection. Say "I understand your concern." The prospect will be impressed you listened. You can then proceed with overcoming the objection.

A great way to overcome objections is the *feel, felt, found technique*. For example, if the prospect says "We are concerned about the mess your workers will cause."

You respond, "I understand how you **feel**." This softens your response and makes them understand you care about their feelings.

You continue, "Many or our best customers **felt** the same way. But they **found** once we completed the installation, we did a thorough clean up. The beautiful new kitchen was worth the inconvenience." *Feel, Felt, Found.*

Remember you do not need to overcome every objection. You only need to overcome enough of the objections so that the value of benefits of your product outweighs the objections.

Overcoming the Price Objection: Is It the Real Issue?

The prospect says your price is too high. Where do you go from here? If you respond with a price-based response, then price is the issue. Many publications claim as many as five out of six prospects will buy quality over price if given the chance. If price is the issue, more often than not it is something in your process that's causing price to be the issue. Is it the salesperson making it or keeping the issue when proper techniques would find out the real issues?

I visited a fabricator in a north suburb of Chicago to show him the Eclipse faucets. After making my presentation, he told me, "Those faucets are great but too expensive for my customer." While I was gathering my samples, a countertop customer came in to return a sample and order her top. As I was putting my samples in their boxes and the customer waited while my prospect printed a copy of the order, she looked over and asked if she could look at the faucets.

I took one of the faucets out of the box and handed it to her. Her first word, like many prospects, was, "Wow." I replied, "You see the Eclipse faucets are solid stainless steel and, unlike most faucets which have a lot of plastic parts, the faucets is heavy." She then said, "Tell me more," so I did. My prospect looked on as I worked through the features and benefits of the faucets never mentioning the price. When I was done, the customer said, "I want it. How much?"

I looked at my prospect because I had no idea what his normal markup might be. My look was met with a small shrug of the shoulders. So I took a chance and quoted a price that was just below 100% mark-up for the fabricator. The customer said,

"Is that all? I was going to pay a lot more for one that is not nearly the quality this one is."

This prospect is now a customer and buys faucets regularly. Later he told me that the markup I quoted was three times his normal mark up on faucets.

There are two important lessons in this story.

1. Never assume you cannot make a sale until you try; and
2. Do not quote a price until the customer WANTS your product.

Are you assuming price is always the issue even when it is not?

Is your advertising bringing you price-only customers? If you are advertising using words like *lowest price* or *cheapest* or advertising an unrealistic low price hoping to sell up once you get in front of the customer, then maybe you are only attracting price-only prospects. If you are attracting price-only prospects, selling up will most often be unsuccessful or cause anger and distrust. Anger and distrust rarely lead to profitable sales and can cause all kinds of bad public relations.

One of my former customers has a sign outside his office advertising a low per- square-foot price for granite. I still visit him occasionally to see if anything has changed. Every time I visit, he spends most of the time complaining about his customers and how they are only interested in price.

A half-mile down the street is a fabricator customer of mine. He never quotes square-foot prices. He likes his customers and he averages almost triple the price posted outside the other fabricator's shop. He lives on referrals and proper sales techniques. Most important, he is always too busy to talk with me for long.

What can you do? Instead of responding to the price issue, ask for clarification. "What do you mean by that?"

If the prospect responds that they can purchase your product for less somewhere else, then you have a chance to review the benefits of your product over the competition, if you *know* the competition. Does the price include everything the customer needs – shipping, setup, warranty? Is the quality the same? Are there other differences that make your product more valuable?

If they say they cannot afford your product, then you can explore that situation. Is that really the issue or do they not want to afford it. Is there a way to make the prospect understand that they cannot afford *not* to buy your product?

Find out what the difference is in the price of your product verses the alternative product. It helps to know your competition's prices because prospects will be confused by pricing and often not know what they are really paying for their product. Prospects will also lie - *they call it negotiating* - about the price of the competition's product.

You do not have to sell the full price of your product; only the difference in price, because they are already buying or have psychologically bought the alternative.

You only need to demonstrate that the value of your product exceeds the difference in price.

Make up a checklist of what to look for from a stone fabricator.

Ask for the Order

Ok so you have gotten to the end of the process and it is time to sum it all up. You need to ask for the order.

There are all kinds of books written on closing. Most imply that you need to trick the customer or at least coax them into buying. These methods even have names: *the Ben Franklin close*, where you make a list of all the pros and cons; *the alternative close* ("Do you want the delivery on Tuesday or Wednesday?); or *the impending event close* (the price goes up on Monday.)

Customers have caught on to many of these closes and may feel manipulated. The best way to close is to create a atmosphere where you are not selling but the customer is buying. If you do the customer will buy, buy again and give referrals.

If you have done everything right so far, then this step is easy. You will want to review the customer's wants and needs, review how your proposal meets the wants and needs, then review the budget they established and how you meet the budget.

For example: "Let's review what we have accomplished. You told me you wanted x, y and z and your budget for these items was $xxx. We have done a to solve x, b to accomplish y and c to meet your need regarding z. The price for accomplishing this is within your budget. Are we ready to proceed?"

Then SHUT UP! Out-wait them and one of two things will happen: They will want to proceed with the purchase or they will come up with new wants and needs. You write up the order or start again.

If they say, "We need to think it over," start with a softening statement: "I understand, this is a big decision." They will not expect this. "Can I ask what you will be considering while you think about it?" This will help you find out if you have missed something or if there is a need or objection you have not met.

Quoting Price on the Phone

I was calling on one of my best customers who is a Midwest granite fabricator. The person I was speaking with, like most of my customers, wears many hats including the role of primary salesperson. We were speaking at her "desk," which happened to be the reception counter. I was adding value and speaking with her on changes in the sink market we believed were coming when her phone rang.

She excused herself and took the call. I was standing only a few feet away so it was impossible *not* to overhear the conversation or at least one side of the conversation.

Near the end of the conversation I heard, "Of course, just fax or email us your kitchen layout and we would be happy to give you a price."

When she hung up, I avoided saying what I wanted to say, which was, "Are you nuts?" Instead I said, "Lucy, how often do you get orders when you send out a quote like that?" Lucy looked at her co-worker at the next desk and together they agreed they could not ever remember getting an order after sending out a quote that way.

"Why do it?" I replied. "You have by far the best showroom in the area for helping your prospects select not only the right countertops for their kitchen but also all the right accessories. You have samples, displays, posters and you can differentiate your product from low-priced and low-quality competition."

"I did it because we always do it," she replied. "What should I have done?"

"What I would have done is tell the caller you do not know the price for her kitchen without finding out more about her, her family, how they are going to use the kitchen, what kind of quality and color they are want. Then I would have tried to schedule an appointment in the design center."

"But people like that will not come into the showroom."

"Lucy, you are right. It is very likely you will not get them to come in. But you told me you never got an order from a faxed in quote. If they do agree to come in, you have a far better chance of converting them than you do by emailing a price based on their sketch. When they collect prices that way, there is only one basis for choosing a contractor and that is *price*. You will never be the lowest price."

Your company has spent a lot of money to make the phone ring. When it rings, you need to get the most out of each ring. If there is nothing to get when the caller is only interested in price, then it is not good practice to waste more time chasing a sale you will likely never get.

If the prospect did come in, they had a chance of selling their quality and value and other important but critical features of their service like having the right insurance, a great warranty and the financial stability to stand behind it. Some customers will only buy price, but those are likely not this fabricator's customers to begin with, so you are not losing them by refusing to give out a price without collecting facts about the prospect and the project.

Quoting square foot prices has the same pitfalls and makes the price the only issue. We used to be asked for square-foot prices on our houses. That question is far more ridiculous in housing than in granite but it gave the customer an easy way that they could understand to compare builders. You need to make a prospect understand that if they want to make the best choice it is not as easy as picking the lowest price.

Follow Up and Ask for Referrals

Once you finish the project, you need to follow up with the customer. You need to talk with them to make sure that you gave them everything you promised. A happy customer is a huge asset. An unhappy one is an even bigger negative. Ask them how you did and then listen. You do not need to encourage complaints, but if they exist, you need to find out.

In a previous section we talked about stopping by to drop off maintenance instructions. Make an appointment. If you did not do the install, personally tell them you want to stop and make sure the installation was done right. This will impress them that you care about them and the quality.

A great technique is to ask them if there is a convenient time you can come and take pictures of their kitchen because you want to enter it into a contest. They will be proud that you want to enter it into a contest and when you show up to take pictures, the kitchen will be clean for you. Bring a picture waiver for them to sign permitting you to use the photo for contests, advertising and promotional purposes. This not only releases you should you use the photo, but makes them think they really got a special kitchen.

If you are afraid to look at the installation or talk to the customer, it is a pretty good bet there is something wrong with your process or product. If you wait until the customer complains, you may never hear the complaint, but the customer's friend and relatives – *your prospects* – will. If there are issues, deal with them. Once you have dealt with any problems, make corrections to your process if necessary to keep it from happening again. Is it a process failure? Is it a personal issue?

Occasionally there may be a customer who cannot be made happy. It would have been best to identify the customer who you cannot please in advance, but once you get into the endless cycle of trying to please the customer, there comes a time to say "stop". If you are genuinely proud of the product, have built the project in accordance with the contract and your standards and done your best, then tell the customer you are done and stop.

We had a customer in our home building business who wanted us to replace her kitchen floor because it was not "pretty enough." Customers like that will never be happy and will never give you referrals. Do the job and do it right, then move on.

Assuming you have built up rapport and done the job right, you have the right to a referral. Ask the customer if they have a friend or relative that they think could benefit from your services. Do not be disappointed if they do not come up with a name right away. Most people will have difficulty when asked to think of someone on a moment's notice.

Leave your maintenance instructions with your cards attached. If they have the instruction in their drawer, they will think of you when someone asks. Other effective reminders are the now-popular refrigerator magnets. If the magnet has helpful information such as a measure conversion chart (quarts/cup/pints, etc.) or first-aid tips, it is even more likely to remain in plain sight.

Things You Need To Know About Your Customer

1. The customer is not always right but they are always the customer. They need to be treated with the respect they deserve.
2. People love to buy but they hate to be sold.
3. Your competitor wants to steal them.
4. People buy emotionally but they want a logical reason to justify the emotional decision.
5. They do not want to understand your product the way you do. They just want it to do what they want it to do when they want it done every time.
6. They want it delivered when they want it and do not care about YOUR delivery problems.
7. They want the warranty to cover all their problems not what the warranty says. They also do not want to read the warranty.
8. They believe they are your best customer and you need them more than they need you.
9. Your customers are afraid of you. They are afraid of being sold.
10. Buyers are not liars but they can have a different and unique perspective, which means they do not always tell the truth.
11. The decision maker (or influencer) may be hidden: mother-in-law, other relatives or friends, for example.
12. Your product does NOT need to be the cheapest but the quality-to-price ratio must be in balance.
13. They may be friendly or even *be* your friend, but they must feel your product is the best solution for their needs or they will buy elsewhere. Relationships are important but they cannot be the only thing that keeps a customer.

Product and service need to be as good as the relationship.
14. The customers who are most excited about your presentation are often those who cannot afford it. They are excited because they are not afraid of being sold.
15. The customers who place orders at the first meeting often cancel and are the hardest to sell because they are easiest to steal.
16. The customer may not need the fastest delivery but they want it when you said they would get it.
17. Not every prospect is *your* customer. You can fire them and sometimes you need to. You cannot afford a bad customer.
18. And remember Truth #1: The customer is not always right but they are always the customer. You need to treat them with the respect they deserve, but it is a two-way street. The sales needs to be good for the customer … and *you*.

Things You Need To Know About Your Market

1. Good or bad, your market will change.
2. Just when you get a feel for the competition and find a strategy to combat them, the competition will adjust.
3. The competition is not always another company. It is often the status quo. Whatever a prospect is doing, it will be hard to get them to make a change.
4. The competition may come from alternate solutions to the problem you solve such as move instead of remodel or alternate uses of the money.
5. Do not rely on your customers for information on your competition. They may not be lying but they may misunderstand or may be "negotiating." This is particularly true when customers quote your competition's price.
6. If the competition does not cause problems, the economy or the government will.
7. The competition will come after your unique selling proposition so you need to be working on the next one.
8. The competition will not fight fair or tell the truth.
9. The market will adjust to the changes you make to your product or marketing faster than you think possible, particularly if you are the leader in your industry or area.
10. Repeat sales are easier than new sales because the risk in the prospect's mind is reduced to near zero.
11. If you let items you cannot control to *control you*, you lose. Bad economy, unfair competition, poor prospects or slow season are not as bad as your perception of them. Take responsibility and overcome the issue.
12. There are opportunities in every negative situation.

Things You Need to Know About Salespeople

1. There are more bad salespeople than professional salespeople.
2. Salespeople can be educated (training is for dogs) but attitude is more important than education because without a sales attitude, the education will do no good.
3. It is an easy low-paying job or a hard high-paying job. It's up to the salesperson.
4. A salesperson cannot learn to get better unless they want to learn, desire to learn and have a passion for learning.
5. If a salesperson stops learning, they lose.
6. Money or high income cannot be the only goal.
7. Being a people person is an admirable trait, but wanting to help people is more admirable. If you help the customer, the rewards will come.
8. Salespeople hate cold calling.
9. Salespeople are paid for results – not activity.
10. It is easy to look busy and not be working. Working is doing something that leads to a sale. A salesperson needs to WORK when they are working.
11. Product and customer knowledge is more important than closing technique.
12. Salespeople chasing a sale to get a commission will likely lose the relationship for future sales … and will likely lose the sale. If a salesperson does the right things at the right times and for the benefit of the customer, sales will come.
13. A good salesperson takes responsibility for all results, good or bad. If a salesperson does not take responsibility, then outside forces that they cannot control (economy, competition, etc) will defeat them. If a salesperson takes responsibility, they can make correction to the process and improve results.

The Hardest Thing in Sales

The hardest thing to do in sales is to learn when to shut up.

You are meeting with a customer and they express a problem. Rather than explore and develop the need, it is understandably tempting to jump in with a solution to that problem. It is more effective to ask probing questions to discover how critical the need is, then decide if it is a problem your product or service can fix.

The customer says that they are unhappy with the deliveries from their current supplier and you jump in with how fast and dependable your deliveries are. What you *should* do is ask, "How does that impact you?" or "Tell me more about that."

Had you asked the question and then shut up, you might have discovered just how critical deliveries are to the customer from a minor annoyance to a game-changing critical need.

It is almost impossible not to jump and vomit your presentation, much less ask a question. And if you *do* get out the question, then it is even harder to wait for the answer.

Customers have been conditioned to wait and let you jump into the quiet. But if you wait, they will answer and when they do, you need to be ready to listen.

Shut up and listen is a critical and nearly impossible skill. Bite your lip, count or whatever it takes to keep from speaking. If you speak first, not only will you lose the moment, but you will have taught your prospect they do not need to answer, but simply wait you out. Only by mastering this skill will you succeed above the average.

If are you asking for the sale indirectly (closing) and do not shut up and listen, you will never know if the technique would have worked. For example: If you ask, "Would you like that in blue or red?" and do not wait for the answer, you are letting the customer choose nothing. You do not get the order AND you do not get any information. If you waited, you might have heard, "We would like it in blue," which would have moved the sales along, or you might have heard, "We need it in shocking pink," which would tell you that you have a problem, assuming you do not have shocking pink. Either way, you have gained. By jumping in, you get nothing.

Four Positive Outcomes of a Sales Call

When you make a sales call, four things can happen. If you do it right, all four will be positive.

The first positive outcome is you make the sale. This is, of course, my favorite outcome but as salespeople, like all-star baseball players, we often fail more often that we succeed.

The second positive outcome is to eliminate the contact from your prospecting list. You may determine the contact is not a good fit for your product. The contact might have a source with which you cannot compete. For example, "I buy from my brother-in-law." You may determine they are more trouble than they are worth. I once worked with a custom home prospect and he and his wife were giving us all the right buying signs. Until he told me that he wanted to do a lot of "due diligence" on my company because he had such a bad experience with his last builder. He also announced he would require a clause with a penalty for late completion.

I asked him who the builder was. He was evasive so I looked up where they lived. I knew the subdivision's builder so I called him to ask about the prospect. His exact words were, "Do not walk away. Run." Turns out this customer had a late penalty in that home purchase contract. The builder was unable to complete the home because the buyer never made the material selections on time but still wanted to enforce the late penalty. We decided that was not a customer we needed.

You may also discover that the prospect cannot or will not pay you. Better to find that out and remove them from your prospect list then make a sale for which you are not paid or have to chase the payment.

The third positive outcome is you get a commitment for a future meeting or move the prospect to the next step in your sales process. In housing, we would try to move a step each meeting: reservation, contract, financing, design, final design and pre-construction meeting. Sometimes there is no commitment, but you build a relationship. In our sink business, I would often have to meet with someone several times, each time building a little more trust. I have a customer it took a year to convert. It took several mini-presentations to build trust. He visited a booth we had at a trade show and I was able to show him all our products and get him to start ordering.

At some point, you will either make the sale or stop making progress, which is when it is time to put the contact into the second category and eliminate them from consideration.

The fourth positive outcome is you do not make the sale, do not eliminate them and do not move the prospect to the next step. In this case you need to analyze the sales call. What did you do right? Where did you screw up? What would you do differently? Is there any way that the outcome could have been different? With this outcome you learn something valuable.

No one makes every sale and everyone screws up a sale they could have made. Even if there was nothing else positive, if you do the right analysis after the meeting, you will have learned something.

Thomas Robinson

Working Home Shows and Trade Shows: Part 1

Shows, whether trade shows for business-to-business sales or a home show directed at gaining consumer business, are similar and have similar strategies.

Recently, I was at a festival where they rented booths to just about any vendor who wanted to pay the rent. There were three different companies selling different devices that attached to gutters to keep out leaves. One had a gutter with their product on display and a number of posters on the product. The salesman sat on a stool reading a magazine. Predictably, no one was coming to his booth to bother him.

At a second booth, a saleslady was standing in front of the booth, flyers in hand. She was dressed in blue jeans and a T-shirt; not at all like the typical upscale prospect. The display was similar to the first but as each potential prospect walked by, she would reach out and attempt to hand each person a brochure and say, "Would you like information on our product?" What few brochures got into prospects' hands wound up in the trash bin at the end of the aisle.

A third had almost no products displayed. What he had was a drawing of a guy falling off a ladder and another of a homeowner with his hand on his back in obvious pain. He would greet people with, "Are you tired of cleaning gutters?" He was still not overwhelmed with customers but he was getting a few to listen to his short presentation and collecting a few names.

- You have to *know the show*. Will the right people be at the show? If you are selling a home improvement product,

are the attendees of the show likely to be in an income range to afford your product? Are the attendees likely to need your product? If the show targets young couples living in apartments, then it is not the right show for your landscaping business. If it is a trade show, is it one your customers are likely to attend? Is it a show aimed at decision makers or staff? Free shows will generally be less successful than shows the prospect needs to spend money to attend.
- You need to work the show! Sitting in your booth and hoping a customer comes up and begs to buy your product is *not* working the show. You need to be on your feet greeting everyone who walks by your booth until you disqualify them as a prospect.
- Start with qualifying questions. "*Hi. Do you hate to clean your gutters?*" or in a business setting, "*What business are you in?*" Get them talking about themselves. The prospect does not care about your company unless there is something in it for him or her. Engage the customer and get information that might help you.
- Arouse interest and get their name. Do not try and close them at the show. Unless you are selling knives or mops that they can buy at the show, doing too much talking and showing too much of your presentation will likely hurt – *not help* – you in the long run. If they think they know everything about the product or service, why should they talk with you again?

Working Home Shows and Trade Shows: Part 2

- A great approach is posing a question. For example if you are selling saunas, "What is the most important thing about owning a new sauna? The customer will likely have no idea. You answer, "The most important thing about owning a sauna is _____." and you fill in the blank with the features or benefits your company is strongest in. You might say, "The most important thing is ease of cleaning and energy efficiency. If we could demonstrate that the XYZ Sauna is the best on the market in ease of cleaning and energy efficiency, would you be interested?"
- Do not waste time with people who will not buy. At every show I have done, there has been at least one person who somehow takes a liking to you and wants to tell you all about how all their friends and relatives use a product just like yours or worse, wants to tell you what is wrong with your product. Be polite but get rid of them.
- At trade shows, you also have the opportunity to talk with existing customers, build rapport and demonstrate new product. Have a plan to deal with the customers. Explain that you need to talk to new customers. At a trade show, I have another employee from my company ready to handle existing customers, show them new products, handle questions and generally entertain them while I greet new customers. Establish in advance who will do what.
- If you can be a speaker at a presentation, it will give you a lot of credibility, even if not everyone you would like attends.

- Do not give out a lot of brochures! Go to the washroom and notice how many big expensive brochures are in the trash. Attendees at shows are unlikely to want to carry armloads of brochures and even if they do, they are unlikely to look at them once they get them home. Give them something small and follow up after the show.
- Have a simple booth that demonstrates your capabilities. A crowded booth looks messy. Almost always a show is prospecting – not selling. Get an appointment for later.
- Have someone shop your competition. You can learn not only about their product but how they sell.
- And you need to follow up as soon as practical after the show. Contact the customer and find out who the good prospects are.

I recently had the opportunity to talk with a couple of customers of mine after they did the same home show. One told me it was a great show and another told me it was a waste of time. Did I mention it was the same show? You need to work the show or it will not work for you.

I Hear You

I am not one who is much for categorizing people, primarily because no matter what the categories are, few people fit neatly into one or the other. Most are some mixture. It is helpful, however, to understand how people make decisions and how people perceive the world.

There are three basic ways that people receive and process information; Auditory, Visual and Kinesthetic.

Auditories will most effectively receive information by hearing it. To deal with an auditory, it is best to make your presentation verbally because that is how they process information. They will say, "I hear you," when they mean "I understand you." With this group, a phone presentation can be as effective as a face-to-face meeting. If you are presenting a contract, it will be most effective to read the important parts out loud to assure understanding.

Visuals will most effectively receive information through pictures. If you are making an oral presentation, they will often be creating pictures in their heads. They may seem to drift off as you are speaking while they create visions in their heads. Eye contact is very important. Presentations with a lot of colorful pictures and graphs will be important as long as you give the prospect time to absorb the picture before you begin the verbal. When presenting written information, it is best to allow the prospect to read it before discussing the information. When they are thinking, their eyes are often looking at the ceiling as they paint the picture of what you are talking about in your head.

Kinetics receive information through *feelings*. Allowing the prospect to feel and touch samples is important. Prospects will make decisions based on instinct and gut feelings. They might say, "It feels right."

In my experience, it is difficult to quickly place individuals into these categories, especially if it is to be of any use in short sales cycles. It is easier to use in longer sales cycles or over longer relationships where there is ongoing or repeat purchases. If you can identify a customer who fits into one of these slots, it will easier to meet their needs and cultivate an ongoing relationship.

Keep the Prospect Engaged

Have you ever been making a presentation and know by the look on the prospect's face that you have lost them? You can almost see them working on other projects while you are talking your heart out with the terrific presentation you spent hours perfecting.

Most people have an attention span of about 30 seconds. If you want to keep the prospect engaged in your presentation, you need to ask them a question every 30 seconds. There are a number of ways you can do this. The easiest is to make a statement a question. For example, instead of saying, "We insulate all the walls with R19 insulation," you can say, "Were you aware that homes that have R19 insulations like ours use 12% less energy?" It's a simple change, but asking a question wakes them up to the fact that they are involved in an interactive event and not just a monologue. When a prospect hears a question, they pay better attention because they understand they may have to respond.

In general, any fact can and should be made as a question. Instead of, "Nickel makes the finish harder," you can say, "Were you aware that nickel in the stainless steel makes the finish harder and last longer?"

Stating benefits as a question can be a particularly effective technique. "Can you see how your family will enjoy the large quiet family room overlooking the back yard?"

You can also insert questions with assumptive answers such as, "Having a large efficient kitchen for everyday use and entertaining is important, isn't it?" You have to be careful with overusing this technique or using it when you are not sure they will agree. You would not like them to interrupt your presentation by saying "No, we never entertain and I hate to clean a big kitchen."

Painting word pictures is also a great way to get them in the moment. The statement above ("… enjoy the large quiet family room" is an example. Another is "Can you see how you car will fit in the large garage?"

In general always ask a fact instead of saying it if you can and paint a picture so they stay engaged.

Thomas Robinson

The Pitch

I hate the term pitch. It brings up a lot the negative stereo types associated with sales from used car salesman to snake oil salesmen but it still is in wide use. If you have been to any home show you have likely seen a pitch selling knives, food processors, mops or some other must-have home gadget.

It is as much show as sales presentation. The mop guy keeps throwing red dye on the floor then showing how he can mop up gallons of water in one pass. He then wrings out the mop and it washes your car, cleans windows and the laundry. The mop is so good the salesperson offers two for the price of one. The pitch is so effective it attracts crowds and as many people in that crowd as not walk away with a mops. The price is relatively low so the sale can be made on the spot.

If you buy this supper mop and take it home it is just a mop. You try to remember why you bought it. If you do not buy the mop you have forgotten about the mop before you get the your car in the parking lot.

If you presentation is like the mop guy you will build excitement and you will be convinced that you've made the sale. You have an excited prospect who may even think they need your product. How can the prospect not want it with all the features and benefits. But unless you have a product you can close at that meeting the excitement will wear off and the next time you call the prospect has entered a five year meeting and will never take your call.

Unless you can close the deal on the spot, a great high-pressure pitch like the home shop mop presentation will not help you. More often than not, it will hurt. In larger, more complicated sales or in sales that depend on repeat business, building excitement with a high-pressure pitch will not work. You need to discover needs and develop solutions to very specific problems that the decision maker has expressed.

To make a great presentation that is memorable and makes the prospect want the product, you need to uncover the prospect's needs and problems and make them part of the presentation. The needs and problems of the prospect do not go away. If you have made the case that your product best solves his or her problems, then every time the problem comes up the prospect is reminded of your solution.

Be a Consultant

In our sink business we have a very big customer who was bidding a large job and needed "special pricing" on lavatory bowls. Rather than chase this sale because I knew there were a number of lower prices, if not lower quality bowls, that might be good enough for a bid job, I spent time with the customer. I told him there were cheaper sinks on the market. I even told him where he could purchase them. I told him the differences between our product, which he used and with which he was familiar, and the lower priced product. I educated him on both products and let him decide which of the products were best for him.

The following Christmas, this customer sent me a holiday gift. I called him to thank him particularly because it is VERY unusual for a salesperson to get a gift from a customer. When I told him this, he remarked, "I do not think of you as a salesman. You are our sink expert. We can rely on you for the right information." He reminded me of the lavatory bowl incident. He said "Your honesty in telling me about the other product did not cost you a sale but it might have. We know we can trust what you tell us."

I earned a loyal customer by not chasing a sale when perhaps there was another product that could meet the customer's needs. Of course, to be a consultant or to do sales as a consultant you have to know your product forward and backward and know the alternative products – not just the competition. You also have to know your customers and their industry. In this case, I needed to know that what alternative products were out there and I needed to understand that price – not quality – was the prime issue in projects that were bid.

Another way to act as a consultant is to share ideas that might help a customer that you learned from another. You need to be careful you are not helping a direct competitor or you might lose the respect and loyalty of both. I had a customer who found an excellent way to use scrap granite. Two states away I had a similar customer who I thought would benefit from the same process. I asked the customer who created the process if he minded if I shared his idea with another customer and I told him where this customer was located.

Not only did he not mind but he was willing to talk with the customer and wound up helping him set up a similar operation. The second customer benefited from the process. There was no possibility that I would get any sales opportunity out of the new process but I gained the customer's respect and loyalty. I also gained the respect and loyalty of the first customer because I had not only listened to him but understood and passed the information on. He was thrilled to be the mentor.

Finding Out What Makes People Buy

If you are going to develop a solution that meets the customer's needs, you need to have an effective way to understand what they really need. Here are a few questions that can help.

1. What process did you go through last time you purchased widgets or selected a widget supplier?
2. What would you do different next time?
3. If you could change one thing about widgets you buy what would it be?
4. How would you improve your present widget solution?
5. When I say widgets what is the first thing that comes to mind? They will often respond with their biggest problem. For example: If they say "late deliveries," then you have an area to work on provided you can fix the problem.
6. What do you look for in a widget?
7. What have you learned about using widgets?
8. What is the most important thing about using, installing or selling widgets?
9. How have you used widgets successfully?
10. What do you do that your competitor does not? How will better widgets help you with that?
11. What does your customer like about your widgets?
12. What do you think your customer would think is valuable?
13. Why do you buy from XYZ or if it is your customer, why do you buy from us? This is particularly effective to ask your existing customers. You may be surprised

why your customer buys from you. You can then use that as a benefit when speaking to prospects. In our sink business, we found several of the prime reasons our customer bought from us had more to do with what we did instead of what we sold.
14. What would you like to see from your account rep?
15. How important is the responsiveness of the sales rep and the rest of the staff to you?
16. What services in addition to supplying widgets would you like from your supplier?
17. What impact would a widget partner, instead of just a supplier, have?
18. How would lowering you inventory help your bottom line?
19. How do you like to order widgets – by the project or do you purchase stock in bulk?

These questions will likely lead to more questions. You need to build on the answers with other questions such as:

- Why do you say that?
- What will that do for you?
- How will that help?
- What is the impact of that on your profits?
- How often does that happen?
- What is the risk of changing suppliers?
- What is the value of solving that problem?

Why Do Your Customers Buy From You?

Why do your customers buy from you? There are likely many reasons customers buy from you but it's not an unlimited number. If you can discover those reasons, you can use them to find and convert more prospects.

When we were selling homes, our customers bought from us because of the locations of our subdivisions. We located them in school districts where there were limited vacant properties for new homes. This was the prime reason they bought. All the quality we knew we built into the home was secondary.

We were starting a second subdivision in a particular school district. We were preparing the marketing material, which included a list of the materials we would be using in the homes in the project. My sales manager came to me with a list of less expensive materials. He said he talked with the customers in the first subdivision and asked them why they bought the homes from us. It was his opinion, based on the discussions with our customers, that we could us less expensive products, some of which the customers would actually prefer, and it would not impact their buying decision.

After a good deal of soul searching, I agreed and among other things, we substituted vinyl siding for cedar, vinyl windows for wood windows with exterior aluminum cladding and standard shingles for premium sculpted shingles.

I was so invested in our materials list that I insisted we offer to upgrade to the original products at our cost. I was convinced that our customers would opt for the materials I thought were better and higher priced.

As the project progressed, we found that the customers actually preferred the vinyl siding to the cedar because they perceived the vinyl siding would require less maintenance. Of the 16 homes in the subdivision, only one opted for the wood windows. When we asked them why, they told us they selected the windows not because of the energy efficiency or longer life of aluminum cladding but because the manufacturer had a color they liked better. No one upgraded to the sculptured shingle.

In this case, our failure to listen to our customers or even discover what they really wanted did not cost us sales, but it did cost us a good deal for options that were of no value to the buying decision.

In the sink business, we interviewed our customers and asked them why the buy from us. We were able to develop a list of 10 reasons. We were surprised to discover that the prime reasons our best customers bought from us had as much to do with quick delivery and customer service as it did with the product.

Who Owns the Customer: Part 1

There are two issues here.

First is where and how is the data stored. Do you and other employees have access to the records? The second is if you rely on a salesperson to manage the relationship with the customer, the customer may perceive the salesperson *is* the company. Are the customers buying from the company or from the salesperson?

In this article we will look at how you store leads and prospect data.

Do you control the prospect lists? Do you have records of sales contacts, face-to-face meetings and phone calls with those prospects?

These lists can be anything from index cards kept in a cardboard box to sophisticated computer programs that not only store the customer and lead info but also keep track of each contact, the status of the sale or the account and a wealth of other information.

The downside of the paper systems is they can be impossible to replace if lost or damaged. Computer programs can be backed up and even duplicated and shared. If your salesperson keeps the paper files, then how do you get access, particularly for outside salespeople? The downside of the more sophisticated programs is they can take a lot of time and energy to manage.

Look at how you keep track of the lists and contacts. Is it appropriate for your business now and can you grow it as the company grows? Is the system uniform or do different salespeople keep their own records their own way? A standardized system will help you fill in for an employee during vacation or illness. It will also help you recover from a resignation or termination.

In our home building business, we allowed our sales people to keep track of their contacts. One project was in a new area, so we decided to employ a local real estate agent with "local knowledge." We built a model home and spent a good deal of money on local advertising.

Sales were below projection, so we asked for a list of prospects from the real estate agent. The agent informed us that the prospects were his property even though we had provided the model and advertising. After terminating this agreement, we were careful to negotiate an arrangement through which we received a weekly prospect list with all information, including the source of the lead.

Who Owns the Customer: Part 2

If you rely on a salesperson to manage the relationship with the customer, the customer may perceive the salesperson *is* the company. I know a situation where a salesperson was let go for cause. When informed by the new salesperson that his predecessor was no longer with the company, several customers asked if he sold the company.

Are the customers buying from the company or from the salesperson? Can your sales person take the customer with them if they move to a competitor?

These are tough questions. You want your salespeople to be outgoing and friendly. You need them to be the face of the company and you want your customers to be comfortable dealing with them. In short, you want the customer to like your salespeople but not more than the company, service or product you are providing.

If your salespeople work from your office, it might be as easy as listening in on few sales calls to see what is being said and how customers are being managed.

If the salespeople are working outside of your immediate place of business, of course, it can be very difficult to find out. You may need to go with the salespeople to see what is happening. Make sure your company's message is consistent and the message you want presented. You may consider written documentation of the message and sales training.

A no-compete-agreement may help, but it may also be unenforceable, particularly if not done at the time you hired the employee.

Do as much as you can to differentiate your company and product from the competition. Find out who your biggest customers are. Call them personally on a regular basis. It only takes a phone call to ask them how they are doing. You may find out some surprising things about your product, your company or your salesperson. Your personal attention will make the customers feel you care about their business and that there is more to your company than just your product.

Thomas Robinson

Conclusion

1. Sales is as necessary to a successful company as making the product. It is an honorable profession.
2. Every employee must understand they are part of the sales process.
3. Sales is a process just like making countertops, even if it seems the outcome is a little less predictable. If professional salespeople do the right thing, at the right time, and for the benefit of the customer, then sales will come.
4. Sales should be a full-time pursuit done by sales professionals – not a part-time job between doing bookkeeping and answering the phone. Given the choice, employees will do easy routine work instead of the hard stuff like cold calling and follow-up calls.
5. Sales is about asking – not telling.

And finally; you cannot learn sales in a seminar or book. You need to listen to seminars and tapes and read books on sales. There are very few new ideas in sales. However, you need to study these experts and *practice, practice, practice.*

Sales is like jazz. You have to learn all the notes and be able to play the instrument. But you have to play it over and over and over to be able to interpret the music, make it work and make it yours.

Tom Robinson
trobinson725@gmail.com

Thomas Robinson

APPENDICES

Articles may be used and reprinted and shared with your customers, as long as they are not altered and the copyright is listed.

How to Buy the Cheapest Granite Countertop

1. Don't ask for insurance. Paying for insurance is expensive and once your top is in, you cannot see your contractor's insurance policy in the top. If one of the workmen gets hurt they can sue you, as the homeowner, if the contractor cannot cover the claim. If the installer damages your house and disappears, there will be no insurance company to stand behind you. Covering these risks costs money, so do not ask for an insurance certificate.

2. Don't visit the shop where your countertop will be built. Well-equipped shops that are clean and efficient are expensive. The cheapest contractors work out of garages, storage warehouses or even fabricate in your driveway where they do not have to pay rent or for expensive equipment to do the job right.

3. Find out if your contractor has a land line for his or her business or works strictly off a cell phone. People who run an office and plan to be around for the long haul like when you need warranty work will have an office and a permanent phone number. The cheap guys will only have a cell phone that can be changed at a moment's notice and no office or location where you can find them when you need warranty work.

4. Don't ask for references.

5. Don't approve the slabs that will actually used in your project. Slabs will be different depending on the lot number and when they were quarried. Getting slabs that match is expensive. Let the contractor find you the most cost-effective slabs.

6. Pay for your slabs at the slab supplier. This will save the middleman charges. It also means the contractor is cut off for credit reasons at the supplier but what do you care if the contractor has credit problems? You won't have warranty problems.

7. Don't ask what grade of granite you are getting. Even if they have the same name, premium and commercial grade slabs can be very different. Having countertops with uniform color and free of blemishes is expensive.

8. Don't ask which direction the veining in the slab will run or where the seams will be. Properly seamed countertops and countertops where the direction of the veining is properly planned are much more expensive.

9. Let the contractor pick the edge finish and put wax on the edges instead of polishing them. Polishing edges takes expensive equipment and a lot of time. Waxing is cheap and you clean it off so you can get the dull natural just sawed look.

10. Make sure you get a "free" sink. Don't ask it if it meets building code or who will handle the warranty. The very cheapest sinks have no manufacturer's name on them so you cannot track down the manufacturer if the contractor disappears. But it was free.

The Scandal of the Free Sink

Not all, but *most,* stainless steel sinks given away as promotions to sell countertops do not meet local building code. If you received a "free sink" with your countertop, it is possible, and even likely, that it is not certified to meet the Uniform Plumbing Code (UPC)®, International Plumbing Code (IPC)® or the National Plumbing Code of Canada (NPC)®. All components of the plumbing system are required to be certified by a third party accredited agency to comply with standards listed in these codes. For example, if you go to your local building supply store, you will notice there is a label on every pipe listing the standards that the pipe meets. This is the certification information. In the case of stainless steel sinks, the standard is ASME A112.19.3.

In the days before the Internet, the components of your plumbing system were sold largely through supply houses. Being in the plumbing industry, these organizations understood and self-policed these requirements. Then came the Internet and anybody could buy anything, certified or not.

Many countertop fabricators, when the market slowed, were looking for a promotion to boost sales. They began giving away a free stainless sink with their countertops. The promotion was so successful that in some markets, the free sink became the standard. Fabricators looking to stay competitive began looking for the cheapest sink they could find to use as these promotional sinks. Many were not aware of the code requirements, and if they did know, they did not care because after all, it was a "free sink." When you give away a free sink, price will trump quality every time.

So how do you know if a sink is certified? That is a difficult question to answer. One of the requirements of the codes is that the sink be marked with the manufacturer's name and model number in a place accessible in the final installation so the sink can be researched. Most accredited agencies also require that the product be marked with the agencies' certification stamp. If the sink is not marked, it does not comply with the code. Marking alone does not mean certification. At least one major supplier to the fabrication industry listed for several years that they were certified when they were not. The best way to find out if you sink is certified is look for the mark and visit the accredited agency's web page and *not* the sink company's website to find out if the manufacturer is listed. You can also ask for copies of the certification from the accredited agency, and not just a statement from the sink company.

Ultimately, why do you care if your sink is not certified? It means the sink has not been tested to meet the standards. It may have impurities that will shorten the life of the sink or even make it unhealthy to use. If may be made of softer steel. It may not have the ingredients that give a stainless steel sink the lustrous finish that is the signature of a high-quality product. Or it may not have the ingredients that harden the finish that make the sink last a lifetime. If it is not tested and certified, who knows what is in your stainless steel sink?

How to Maintain Your Stone Countertop

Natural stone countertops are a beautiful addition to your home. With proper maintenance they will last a lifetime.

- Next to diamonds, granite is the hardest material in nature. Marble, limestone and other stones offer the same beauty but can be softer and more susceptible to stains and etching, so more care may be necessary.
- Your countertop has most likely been sealed. Sealers are different and have to be reapplied at different intervals. Follow the manufacturer's instructions but if water soaks into the top instead of beading up on the surface, it needs to be resealed.
- Wipe up all spills as soon as possible – particularly acidic liquids like orange juice and white wine.
- Do not use abrasive cleaners or acidic cleaners. They may dull or mar the surface. Cleaners with a balanceed pH are best.
- Cutting directly on the top will likely not damage the granite but might put micro scratches in the finish and dull the surface. You will also wind up with dull knives.
- The countertop will not usually be damaged by heat but because the slab is thin, it may not absorb all the heat from a hot dish. It is best to use a heat pad under hot dishes.
- If you see a dull or rough patch, call your countertop fabricator. It is likely that etching can be repaired.
- Use coasters for drinks.
- Stains, if they occur, can often be removed but it is best to consult with your fabricator.

Thomas Robinson

Granite, Marble and Other Stones

Customers are most often confused about the difference between granite and marble. You can find many articles on each with detailed descriptions of the differences. For example, granite is an igneous rock and marble is a metamorphic rock, which means that granite is solidified from molten magma and marble is rock that was once another form of rock and changed under the influence of heat and pressure.

What does this mean when talking to a customer? Unless you are talking to an engineer or geologist, likely nothing. What you need to know is the differences that your customers understand.

Appearance: The characteristic "spots" on granite are caused by the rocks melting within the stone from the molten state. Marble is usually grayish white or cream or ivory in color with dark veins running through it. These are generalizations and there are many variations.

Granite is harder and more resistant to acids in food and harder to scratch. Marble is softer and requires more maintenance.

Marble is not recommended for outdoor use without sealant.

Both can be damaged by harsh cleaning products but granite is generally more difficult to damage.

Both are more porous than manmade stones like quartz.

Both are heat-resistant and can be stained.

Marble was the stone of choice for small fabricators before better cutting and polishing tools became generally available because it is softer and easier to fabricate. Granite is better for kitchen countertops because they are subjected to high use. Marble is better used in lower traffic areas.

Commercially available stone is classified by how it performs and behaves, not into scientifically defined groups. These groups are: Granite, Limestone, Marble, Onyx, Quartzite, Sandstone, Serpentine, Slate, Soapstone, and Travertine. This means that some stones sold as one group may scientifically fit into a different group.

The most common stones used in countertops are granite and marble. The Marble Institute of America recognizes three different definitions for granite:

Granite: *A very hard, crystalline, igneous rock, gray to pink in color, composed of feldspar, quartz, and lesser amounts of dark ferromagnesium materials. Gneiss and black "granites" are similar to true granites in structure and texture, but are composed of different minerals.*

Granite (commercial definition): *A term that includes granite (as defined below) plus gneiss, gneissic granite, granite gneiss, and the rock species known to petrologists as syenite, monzonite, and granodiorite, species intermediate between them, the gneissic varieties and gneisses of corresponding mineralogic compositions and the corresponding varieties of porphyritic textures. The term commercial granite shall also include other feldspathic crystalline rocks of similar textures, containing minor amounts of accessory minerals, used for speciadecorative purposes, and known to petrologists as anorthosite and larvikite.*

Granite (scientific definition) *A visibly granular, crystalline rock of predominantly interlocking texture composed essentially of alkalic feldspars and quartz. Feldspar is generally present in excess of quartz, and accessory minerals (chiefly micas, hornblende, or more rarely pyroxene) are commonly present. The alkalic feldspars may be present (1) as individual mineral species, (2) as isomorphous or mechanical intergrowths with each other, or (3) as chemical intergrowths with the lime feldspar molecule, but 80 + 3% of the feldspar must be composed of the potash or soda feldspar molecules.*

Similar definitions for other stone can be found on the Marble Institute of America website.

The point is, what may be commercially called one thing may be scientifically called another. Do not get hung up in definitions but rather understand that commercial definitions are based on how the stone performs and not how it looks under a microscope.

The Marble Institute

One of the best sources of reliable information on the stone countertop industry is the Marble Institute of America (www.marble-institute.com).

The Institute has a page set up for consumers that provides a wealth of information. Consumers are more informed than ever and your customers will often come to your showroom after spending hours researching your product. Remember, once things go bad, they might find information that contradicts information you have given them.

You need to study these pages to see what one of the most respected industry sources says about what you do. There is a page showing countertop edges. Your company might not offer all these edges for a number of reasons. Some edges might be problematic, require special tooling that your company does not have or prefers not to offer because they are too expensive. If there are edges that you do not offer, it would likely be helpful if you discover why you do not offer them so you can respond quickly and effectively should the topic come up. Remember, too, that if you have edges *not shown*, it might be a good unique selling proposition for you to use.

There are articles with which you might not agree. For example, there is an article on sealing stone countertops. The article starts with the sentence "*Most granite countertops do not need to be sealed.*" If you are selling and recommending sealers, this would be a good article to read and understand because later in the article, it states, "*In many cases it makes sense to seal marble and granite countertops with a quality sealer.*"

Thomas Robinson

Ten Questions to Ask Your Customers

A prospect wanders into your showroom and immediately walks over to your granite samples on the wall. Your salesperson walks up and says, "That's one of our most expensive stones. Isn't it beautiful?"

You spent money on your showroom, the salesperson, and maybe advertising and all the customer heard was MOST EXPENSIVE.

The best way to convert the customer is to engage them in conversation that INTERESTS THEM!!! A sales pitch will turn them off.

What is the best way to do that? Build rapport and ask questions.

When the customer walks in, greet them with "Hi, my name is Sally," unless your name is not Sally. Then use your name. "Welcome to the Granite Showroom, where we specialize in meeting your needs. What brings you to our showroom today?" You all have granite in your company name somewhere.

The question will lead to many possible answers. The answers will give you insight into their needs and give you a heads up on your competition, which just let them look at stone samples. They may say, "We are selling our house and the real estate agent told us it would sell better with granite countertops." This tells you budget will be the primary concern. Your response will be far different than it will be if they say, "We have just retired and have decided to stay in our house but we want to fix it up so we can stay there the next 20 years."

Selling Stone Countertops

What if they say, "We received a price from the other granite guy in town and are looking to get a better price?" This gives you the opportunity to get information on the quote they have and allow you to sell quality over price if you can.

Here is a list of questions that you can use as a starting point to create your own questions.

1. What brings you to our showroom today?
2. What are you trying to accomplish?
3. What do you have now? Material? Color?
4. What do you like about what you have now?
5. What don't you like about what you have now?
6. How do you use the countertop/kitchen?
7. Why do you believe you want a stone top?
8. What do you expect from a stone countertop? What have family and friends told you about stone tops?
9. What colors do you have in your kitchen/bath/bar? Will you be changing anything else in the room?
10. Do you have a budget in mind for your project?

These are open-ended questions that get them talking so you can gather information.

These are not all the questions you can ask and may not even be the best questions. Develop your own and use them because sales is about asking, not telling. If you find out what the customer wants, you can create a proposal based on their needs. And that leads to more sales.

Thomas Robinson

Ten responses to "What's Your Square-Foot Price?"

1. What quality countertop do you want, the $29-per-square-foot one or a good one?
2. Have you selected a stone? We have commercial seconds from a few dollars a square foot to our precious stone collection that can be hundreds of dollars a square foot.
3. Would you like a warranty that you can count on or can we give you our cell number as the only contact number so we can change it if we have to?
4. Do you want all your slabs to match?
5. Do you want to select the actual slabs that will be used in your countertop or do you want to let us find slabs from different lots that are cheaper because they do not match?
6. Do you want all the directional slab grain to run in the same direction?
7. Do you want us to polish the edges or can we just use wax which will wash off in a few weeks leaving the fresh sawed look?
8. How tight do you want the seams?
9. Do you want us to have insurance or are you willing to risk it if something is damaged or one of our workers is hurt on your property?
10. Would you like us to make the countertop in our shop and deliver it to you, or can we do it in your driveway using your water and leaving traces of granite dust all over your drive and yard?

Selling Stone Countertops

This Booklet was prepared as a written companion to the presentation "A Sales Seminar for Stone Fabricators Who Hate Sales," which was presented at the Stone Fabricators Alliance Megaworkshop in Nashville, TN, in October of 2012. The Seminar and Booklet are sponsored by:

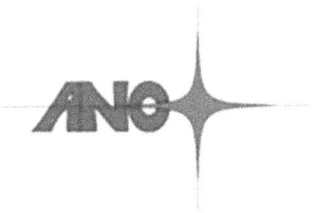

ANO, Inc.
Midwest Distributor of Eclipse Stainless

Partnering with Stone Fabricators to Make Money and Not Have Problems Selling Sinks and Faucets

ANO, Inc.
Arlington Heights, IL
www.anosales.com
847-749-0208
main@anosales.com

Thomas Robinson

About the Author

Tom Robinson is a former land developer and home builder who created and SOLD over $200 million in real estate. He is past president of the Home Builders Association of Greater Chicago and currently director of business development for ANO, Inc. in Arlington Heights, IL. He is author of "May I Borrow Your Watch?" which is available on Amazon.com or by visiting www.robdev.com.

Thomas Robinson

Recommended reading and listening

The number of great books and tapes on sales is endless but here is where I would start.

Selling for Dummies - Tom Hopkins
> Tom Hopkins' greatest expertise is real estate but a lot can be applied to other areas.

Sales Mastery Academy - Zig Ziglar
> Most of the Ziglar 's writing is as much motivational as sales techniques. Both are important as keeping motivated in sales is critical.

High Trust Selling - Todd Duncan
> I particularly liked the discussion on selling more to fewer customers.

Close the Deal - Sandler Sales Institute
> The first time I listened to this series I thought it was very anti-customer and presented sales as a fight. They do, however, say sales is the music but you need to play it your way. There is a lot of value in here regarding process, but you need to study it to discover when to follow it exactly and when to improvise.

Endless Referrals - Bob Burg
> The list of questions to ask when you meet someone is particularly good and can be used in other areas besides networking.

www.ingramcontent.com/pod-product-compliance
Lightning Source LLC
Chambersburg PA
CBHW061514180526
45171CB00001B/176